THE ORIGINAL COCKTAIL BOOK

Classic and Modern Cocktail Recipes for Everyday Enjoyment incl. Gin, Whiskey, Rum, Non-Alcoholic & More

Bernie Morrison

ISBN - 9798839092457

TABLE OF CONTENTS

INTRODUCTION

You do not have to be a mixologist to create a fantastic cocktail. In this book, I will show you simple and effective ways to make cocktails that blow your mind and enchant your senses.

Cocktails do not have to be full of ingredients or cost the earth to create. Sometimes, as with cooking, the simplest cocktail recipes are the best. It is all about combining subtle flavours and mixing methods to make something that looks and tastes amazing.

That said, sometimes it is also a fun challenge to make and drink a complex cocktail, so I have made sure to include a few of those recipes too. From the classic cocktail to the most ornate, this book has everything you need to get you set off on your journey to pure mixology bliss.

When you see a cocktail in a bar that is colourful, whimsical or has that something extra they often cost the earth to buy. Even the standard cocktails can sometimes reach lofty heights when it comes to price. But cocktail bar owners do not have the money to spend on expensive ingredients for everyday customers. There are secret tricks of the trade that I will let you in on to help you make incredible, affordable cocktails at home.

To mix a great cocktail you need three things, love, skill and the right ingredients. This book will take you on a journey of cocktail mixology. I have organised the recipes by the core alcohol they use for the cocktail. This will enable you to easily flick to the recipe you need when you are creating your masterpiece at home.

Create cocktails for your friends and family, at parties and even for your Sunday brunch. This recipe book has it all. If you have never mixed a cocktail in your life, this book is for you. We delve not just into the making of the cocktails but into the history itself.

Give your guests a tour of the decadent, and sometimes downright funny world of cocktails across time. Delve beneath the surface of traditional cocktail creation and try new cocktails that have never been tasted by the public before. Be inspired to create your own unique mix and learn about how to use flavour combinations to create distinct cocktails that will tempt even your most traditional guests.

This book has a section dedicated to non-alcoholic cocktails - to ensure that no one feels left out of the party. Wow your friends and family with recipes that will knock their socks off even if they aren't wearing any. Explore the ingredients that can change your virgin cocktail from a fruit smoothy to an alcohol-free delight.

The Original Cocktail Book will equip you with everything you need to make a big impression. From the equipment and glass sizing to ingredients and measurements. Once you have finished this recipe book you will be the regent of mixology. So come, delve inside the pages and gain that knowledge you have wondered about all your life...

EQUIPMENT

In order to start yourself off as an at-home mixologist, you are going to need some basic equipment. This does not have to be top of the range or expensive. Local supermarkets often have a section dedicated to the growing trend of home-mixology. You can pick up the tools of the trade for low prices and still create beautiful-looking cocktails for your friends and family – and yourself, of course!

Ensure that the equipment you buy is dishwasher safe and sturdy enough to compete with the amount you will be using it once you get started into this new hobby. Some shops sell very cheap products, but they can often rust or fall apart on first use. Therefore, it is important that you buy from a reputable provider such as a major supermarket or home wear shop.

If you want top-of-the-range items, there are retailers online who have some amazing products. There are tools and utensils for specific requirements, including channel knives for paring fruit and even spherical ice makers to ensure your drink stays cold for as long as possible.

There are many alternatives for these items that you might already have in your kitchen so if you are on a budget, have a look around and get creative.

COCKTAIL SHAKER

Professional mixologists often go for the Boston Shaker. It is a 12- or 28-ounce mixing tin that leaves ample room for your drink and ice to be shaken effectively. The top metal tin fits inside the bottom, making it easy to shake and remove. A stainless-steel cocktail shaker is a great idea, as it is durable and chills quickly for the cocktails that you need to be ice cold. Of course, you can also get glass or even ceramic shakers dependent on your preferences. Some home bartenders prefer to go for a shaker with a cap to prevent spillages. These are usually a much cheaper alternative but watch out that it doesn't leak.

HAWTHORNE STRAINER

These strainers fit over your cocktail shaker and are especially useful if you have a two-piece Boston-style shaker. They are designed to catch not only the contents of the cocktail that you do not want in the class but the ice that is in the shaker. They are invaluably useful, if you only get one strainer then opt for this.

JULEP STRAINER

The Julep strainer is designed to fit on the top of your glass. These can be great if you have a shaker with an inbuilt strainer and so don't need a Hawthorne strainer, as it gets rid of any pieces that might have slipped through on the first strain.

FINE STRAINER

The fine strainer helps create the perfect cocktail as it removes the smaller pieces of ice out of your final cocktail, so that they don't float on the top giving your drink that classy finesse.

(you can also use a tea strainer which is just as effective)

MIXING GLASS

You can either opt for a glass or metal mixing glass to use for your home bartending, or you can just use the base of your cocktail shaker for the same effect. It depends on how much you want to spend on your setup.

STIRRING SPOON

Before buying a stirring spoon, measure your mixing glass. You want your spoon to easily reach to the bottom of it so that you can effectively stir your cocktails to the optimum amount. There are many styles of spoon in the market. Choose one that you would like to use, this is where you can start to be creative and put your own stamp on your home bar.

MEASURE

Your measure is important. It should be accurate; otherwise the cocktails will not taste right. You can buy a Jigger measure inexpensively. The Jigger measure is dipped at the bottom and provides a very accurate judge of the liquid that you are adding. Alternatively, use a shot glass though these can be inaccurate.

KNIFE

A knife is a crucial part of the tool kit. You can use standard kitchen knives but ensure they are sharp enough to easily cut through the skin of your lemons and watermelons. This knife will be used for creating garnishes so it being sharp means it will create clean edges and your cocktails will look much more professional. If you are only using one knife for your set up, I suggest a sharp metal knife that is 4 – 6 inches long. This means that it is the right size for larger fruits and for dexterous work with garnishes.

CHOPPING BOARD

An easy to clean chopping board is needed when making cocktails. Wooden boards can be a good option as they are less likely to blunt your knives than glass.

CITRUS JUICER

Ensure you have a citrus juicer that has a drip tray to catch the unwanted pulp from your fruits. You can just use your hands and put it through a strainer.

PEELER, CHANNEL KNIFE AND ZESTER

You might find one or more of these in your kitchen drawer already. They are not absolutely necessary as a grater, or a knife can do a similar job. Consider how well equipped you want your home bar to be and how professional looking you prefer your cocktails.

CORKSCREW

A good corkscrew with an inbuilt bottle opener is fine for cocktail making. It means you can easily interchange when making drinks.

ICE TRAY

You need a lot of ice when it comes to making cocktails. It is entirely up to you if you buy pre-made ice or create the ice in a tray. Different sizes of ice look better with different cocktails. You might want large pieces of ice for an Old Fashioned or crushed for some longer cocktails like a Tom Collins or Long Island. It is also dependent on the size and delicacy of your glass. Putting large cubes of ice in a Martini glass would probably not be a great idea and would certainly make for a poor drinking experience.

ICE SCOOP/ICE BUCKET IN FREEZER

A metal ice scoop is a hygienic way to deal with your ice cubes.

MUDDLER

There are a number of styles of muddler in the market. A muddler acts as a pestle to release the flavours from fresh ingredients that you might add to your cocktails. Not all cocktails require a muddler, of course, and you can get by with using the end of a rolling pin or a similar implement.

NUTMEG GRATER/POWDER SHAKER

A nutmeg grater is a little finer sharper than a standard grater. However, the regular type will do the same job if you don't want to splash out.

The powder shaker is to create a dusted top to a cocktail like those seen on coffees and hot drinks in famous coffee shops. You can also use a teaspoon and lightly shake over the dust by hand.

TEA TOWELS

Always have several clean, dry tea towels to hand when creating cocktails.

ICE CRUSHER

You can buy an expensive ice crusher or alternatively, you can use a mallet, a plastic bag and a tea towel. Put the ice cubes in the bag and wrap in the tea towel. Place on your chopping board and hit with the mallet until they are crushed.

SAUCEPAN AND FUNNEL

A saucepan is needed if you will be melting sugar for your cocktails or making any syrups. If you do get one, ensure it has a lip to allow for ease of pour. The funnel should be metal, so you can feed the finished product into a bottle or jar for storage.

BLENDER

A powerful blender can make all the difference when making cocktails. Pina Coladas, Daiquiris or Bellinis are all best served out of a blender. It means you can really mix the ingredients and create a cocktail infused with fresh fruit, without having it floating in the glass and lessening the rich experience.

Cocktail Sticks – For use with a garnish

Cocktail Umbrellas and other fripperies

Cocktail straws of various sizes.

BASIC INGREDIENTS FOR YOUR HOME-BAR

With these ingredients you can create most of the cocktails listed in this book. Here we have stated those ingredients that come up many times during the progress of the book. Of course, buying them all might cost a small fortune, so you may prefer to go directly to the recipe for your ingredients list – that is totally up to you!

    Simple Syrup – you can also often use sugar if you do not have Simple Syrup available.

Making your own simple syrup is very easy to do. Follow these short steps to make a batch and store it for when you need to use it.

Simple Syrup Recipe:

Ingredients:

Sugar Water

1. Take a 1:1 ratio of water and white sugar.

2. Stir the sugar into hot water (it does not have to boil).

3. Allow it to cool.

4. Pour into a container and refrigerate to store.

Once you have mastered the simple syrup recipe, you can experiment with different sugars (keeping the same ratio). There are other easily made syrups you can create at home.

Orange Syrup Recipe:

Sugar Water Orange Peel

1. Add the ingredients to a pan and stir.

2. Bring to the boil, stirring occasionally.

3. Remove from heat once sugar has dissolved.

4. Leave to cool and combine.

5. Strain into a container and refrigerate to store.

Ginger Syrup Recipe:

Sugar Water Ginger Root

1. Peel and thinly slice or grate the ginger root.

2. Add the ingredients to a pan and stir.

3. Bring to the boil until the sugar has dissolved.

4. Simmer for 5 minutes and continually stir (ensure it is not so hot it burns the sugars).

5. Remove pan from heat and leave to cool and combine (leaving the lid on).

6. Strain into container once cooled and refrigerate to store.

ｚ **Citrus Fruit**: Lemons, Limes, Oranges

You can also keep bottles of lemon and lime juice that you buy from the supermarket as a great back up tool in your home-bar.

We keep citrus fruit at the ready for including in the base of cocktails, but also for its peel, which we use as a garnish.

Creating a citrus twist is a simple and effective way to give your cocktail something extra. Use a lemon, lime or orange to create a beautiful garnish for your drink. You can also run the peel across the rim of the cocktail glass before you twist it to give something extra to the way you serve.

HOW TO MAKE A CITRUS FRUIT TWIST:

Step 1: Cut the end off your citrus fruit.

Step 2: Cut the other end off your citrus fruit.

Step 3: Cut laterally down into the fruit to remove the fruit itself.

Step 4: Cut one lateral line down one side of the skin. You should have a C shaped piece of skin.

Step 5: Cut your twists. Cut into your skin in the opposite direction to create more C shapes, make these the size you want your twists to be.

Step 6: Twist it with your fingers like wringing out a tiny towel.

Step 7: Hey Presto! You have a citrus twist!

🍸 **Maraschino Cherries**

Mint Plant – There are many types of mint out there, also herbs and specialised cocktail sections in some garden centres. Why not go and take a look and see what you can find. You might find a new flavour to add to your cocktails as a syrup, muddle or garnish.

Soda water

Tonic water

Frozen Cranberries

Frozen Strawberries

HOW TO SERVE A COCKTAIL

There are methods to mixing and serving a quality cocktail that you can follow as a home mixologist to impress your guests – and yourself! These are the best tips for creating a quality cocktail with perfect finesse.

- Read and practice the recipe ahead of time and be sure you know which ice, glass and garnish you will need.

- Shake the cocktail shaker up and down and then forwards and backward. Have a practice with ice and water to achieve the stylish pizzazz of a true mixologist.

- Never use the ice in the shaker more than once as it dilutes the drink.

- You can use the ice in a cocktail mixing glass twice but no more than this for the same reason.

- Do not over-pour your cocktails. Always make sure there is enough room in the top of the glass to ensure elegance.

- Serve the cocktails immediately as you pour them from the shaker to enhance the quality.

COCKTAIL GLASS NAMES AND SIZING:

Glass Name	Description	Ml	Oz
Highball	Tall skinny glass	240 – 350 ml	8 – 12 fl oz
Collins	Tall glass	300 – 410 ml	10 – 14 fl oz
Rocks Glass	Small tumbler	180 – 300 ml	6 – 10 fl oz
Champagne Flute	Tall flute shaped	170 – 190 ml	6 fl oz
Coupe	Broad saucer, stemmed	180 – 240 ml	6 – 8 fl oz
Cocktail/ Martini Glass	Wide mouth, conical, stemmed	250 ml	8 – 9 fl oz
Copa de Balon	Bulbous, large, stemmed	800 ml	27 fl oz
Poco Grande	Large double bowl, stemmed	470 – 500 ml	17 fl oz
Hurricane Glass	Tall double bowl, short stem	590 ml	20 fl oz

These are average sizes to go by to help, glass sizes differ dramatically. You can check the size of your glasses at home and see which match up to the recipes in this book.

RECIPES

GIN BASED COCKTAIL RECIPES

Gin makes a fine cocktail alcohol base. A good gin is made with juniper berries. Many supermarket brands are made only from vodka with gin flavouring so if you want the authentic taste make sure you check the label before purchasing.

Flavoured gins are becoming ever more popular, with distilleries around the world creating new and different essences for gin lovers everywhere. There is no reason that these flavoured gins cannot be substituted in various cocktails. Moving away from the traditional and putting your own stamp on it is what makes a great mixologist.

GIN AND TONIC

A Gin and Tonic is a simple and refreshing cocktail that is easy to make and delicious. The important part to master is the balance between the bitterness of the tonic and the flavour of the gin.

INGREDIENTS:

◆ Well Chilled Gin (90 ml // 3 oz)

◆ Tonic Water (120 ml // 4 oz)

GARNISH:

◆ Lime Slice

GLASS AND ICE:

◆ Copa De Balon

◆ Ice Cubes

METHOD:

1. Copa de Balon glass with cubed ice.

2. Pour over your measure of gin.

3. Add the tonic water and stir gently.

4. Place your lime slice on top.

5. Serve.

HINTS AND TIPS:

Improve the flavour of your Gin and Tonic by adding chopped tarragon or 15 ml // ½ oz of lime juice.

DRY MARTINI

The Dry Martini is one of the best-known and loved styles of martini. Invented over one hundred years ago, it gets its name from the low levels of vermouth that are added to balance out the flavour of the gin.

INGREDIENTS:

- ◆ Dry Gin (60 ml // 2 oz)
- ◆ Dry Vermouth (15 ml // ½ oz)

GARNISH:

- ◆ An olive

GLASS AND ICE:

- ◆ Martini/Cocktail glass, chilled

METHOD:

1. Fill your mixing glass with ice and add the gin and vermouth.

2. Stir for 20 seconds.

3. Pour into a martini glass over a strainer.

4. Garnish with an olive and serve.

HINTS AND TIPS:

There are so many ways to have a martini. Once you have mastered this, why not try some different Martini recipes using herbal flavours.

NEGRONI

The Negroni is an Italian classic. It is said it was borne after Count Camillo Negroni asked for his favourite cocktail, the Milano – Torino, to be strengthened with gin. It is a classic drink with a strong flavour and one that is very enjoyable to test out at home with its moreish qualities.

INGREDIENTS:

- Gin (30 ml // 1 oz)

- Campari (30 ml // 1 oz)

- Vermouth (30 ml // 1 oz)

GARNISH:

- Orange Peel

GLASS AND ICE:

- Rocks Glass

- Ice Cubes

METHOD:

1. Add the gin, Campari and Vermouth to a mixing glass and stir for one minute to ensure they are fully chilled.

2. Strain over a rocks glass with ice cubes.

3. Add the orange peel garnish.

4. Serve.

HINTS AND TIPS:

Add Champagne or Prosecco to dilute the strong flavours, or a squeeze of fresh lime to add sourness.

FRENCH 75

The French 75 should always be served in a champagne flute. Known for its strong kick, the French 75 is so called after a French gun used in the First World War that hit with incredible speed and accuracy.

INGREDIENTS:

- Gin (45 ml // 1 ½ oz)

- Chilled Champagne (90 ml // 3 oz)

- Fresh Lime Juice (20 ml // 2/3 oz)

- Simple Syrup (20 ml // 2/3 oz)

GARNISH:

- Lemon Peel

GLASS AND ICE:

- Champagne flute, chilled.

METHOD:

1. Fill a cocktail shaker with ice and add the gin, lemon juice and simple syrup.

2. Shake well for twenty seconds.

3. Strain into champagne flutes.

4. Top with champagne.

5. Garnish with lemon peel and serve.

HINTS AND TIPS:

Add elderflower or rose syrup for added finesse.

GIMLET

The Gimlet was drunk by British Officers in the 19th Century. Lime juice was given to sailors in a ration, as the vitamin C that it contained helped prevent scurvy. The sailors mixed the lime juice with their daily rum-based grog, a concoction known as a 'Limey'. The navy officers received rations of gin, and so, it is said that this was the origin of Gimlets. However, no one knows for sure.

INGREDIENTS:

- ◆ Gin (60 ml // 2 oz)
- ◆ Lime Cordial (30 ml // 1 oz)
- ◆ Fresh Lemon Juice (10 ml // 1/3 oz)

GARNISH:

- ◆ Maraschino Cherry

GLASS AND ICE:

- ◆ Coupe Glass, chilled

METHOD:

1. Add gin, like and lemon juice to a cocktail shaker filled with ice.

2. Shake for 20 seconds.

3. Strain into a Coupe glass.

4. Add maraschino cherry garnish.

5. Serve.

HINTS AND TIPS:

Adding fresh basil can bring the Gimlet alive. While the drink is still in the shaker, add a handful of fresh basil. Use a muddler to draw out the flavour and strain. Serve as for a regular Gimlet.

TOM COLLINS

The Tom Collins was first recorded in 1875 when it appeared in the book 'The Bartender's Guide' by Jerry Thomas. There are many arguments about the origin of the drink's name. Some say it is after an American HOAX with a gentleman named Tom Collins in 1974 - who never existed. It was a joke told in bars to trick people into thinking a rude gentleman named Tom Collins spoke negatively about them. They would storm off and look for him, while the rest of the bar thought it was a jolly funny ruse.

INGREDIENTS:

◆ Dry Gin (60 ml // 2 oz)

◆ Lemon Juice (30 ml // 1 oz)

◆ Simple Syrup (15 ml // ½ oz)

◆ Club Soda to top

GARNISH:

◆ Lemon Wheel

◆ Maraschino Cherry

GLASS AND ICE:

- ◆ Collins Glass
- ◆ Ice Cubes

METHOD:

1. Stir gin, lemon juice and simple syrup in a mixing glass with ice until chilled.

2. Fill a Collins Glass with ice and strain in the mix.

3. Top with club soda and gently stir.

4. Add lemon wheel and cherry as a garnish on a cocktail stick.

5. Serve.

HINTS AND TIPS:

A Tom Collins tastes great with a demerara sugar syrup. Follow the same recipe as for simple syrup but replace the sugar with demerara.

If you want to try something different try adding a piece of stem ginger as a garnish to give it a bite of sugary fire.

WHISKEY-BASED COCKTAIL RECIPES

Whisky can be made of a variety of grains including, rye, corn, wheat and barley. It originated as a medicine, both internally as an aesthetic and externally as an antibiotic. Its usage changed around 1100 when monks started distilling whisky in Ireland. The variety of bases in a whisky, and the time it is left to mature make the difference in flavour from a light tangy flavour to a deep smoked oak whisky.

The whisky cocktail is one of the oldest variations of cocktail recipe, and they are still just as popular today with many patrons choosing a whisky cocktail over any other.

A budding mixologist should be able to mix a whisky-based cocktail that highlights the flavour of the whisky itself and blends it with minimal flavours to create a taste experience. In this chapter we will take you through the world of whisky based cocktails and show you how to create these historical beacons in your own home.

OLD FASHIONED

The Old Fashioned was arguably invented by James E. Pepper in 1881. It wasn't until much later that it was named 'The Old Fashioned' due to the number of gentlemen who refused to change with the modern times and liked to order their cocktails the old way - with a brown liquor, sugar cube and bitters.

INGREDIENTS:

- Bourbon (60 ml // 2 oz)

- Bitters, 3 dashes

- 1 sugar cube

- Water, tablespoon

GARNISH:

- Orange peel

GLASS AND ICE:

- Rocks Glass

- Ice Cubes

METHOD:

1. Add sugar and bitters direct to your rocks glass.

2. Add water and stir until the sugar is dissolved.

3. Add ice and bourbon.

4. Stir gently.

5. Add orange peel garnish and serve.

HINTS AND TIPS:

Squeeze the orange peel over the glass to add the oils to the flavour.

Create with simple syrup and maraschino cherries to make a sweeter Old Fashioned.

WHISKEY SOUR

The Whisky Sour is another old sailor's drink. To prevent sailors from becoming too intoxicated and to spread alcohol rations, their whisky was watered down. As with the Gimlet, fresh lemon juice would have been added to combat outbreaks of scurvy. The first printed record of the Whisky Sour was in the book 'How to Mix Drinks' by Jerry Thomas in 1862, but it is very likely that it dates back to far earlier times.

INGREDIENTS:

♦ Bourbon (60 ml // 2 oz)

♦ Fresh lemon juice (10 ml // 1/3 oz)

♦ Simple Syrup (10 ml // 1/3 oz)

GARNISH:

♦ Orange Wheel

GLASS AND ICE:

♦ Rocks Glass

♦ Ice Cubes

METHOD:

1. Add bourbon, lemon juice and simple syrup to a cocktail shaker.

2. Fill shaker with ice.

3. Shake vigorously for 20 seconds.

4. Strain into a rocks glass.

5. Add orange wheel garnish.

6. Serve.

HINTS AND TIPS:

Whisky sours can be made using a variety of flavours and still hold the same great taste. Choose a flavoured syrup to add and change the garnish accordingly. We suggest cherry syrup with a maraschino cherry syrup if you like it sweet. Or a mint syrup with a sprig of mint leaves if you prefer a tarter flavour pallet.

MANHATTAN

There are arguments over who invented the Manhattan. It was served at a banquet party involving Winston Churchill's mother and many people say it came from there. Another by a man named Blacks who lived in Manhattan. However, off the coast of Denmark on the Friesen Islands, they drink a drink that looks very much like a Manhattan as a traditional beverage. Many Friesians emigrated to the US and to Manhattan on fishing trips. The story goes that they loved the drink and took it back with them, but who knows, it might just be that they took it to Manhattan in the first place!

INGREDIENTS:

- Bourbon Whisky (60 ml // 2 oz)
- Sweet Vermouth (30 ml // 1 oz) ~Sausbys
- Bitters, 2 dashes
- Orange syrup (10 ml // 1/3 oz)
  Oranges

Cocktail sticks

GARNISH:

- Brandied Cherry

GLASS AND ICE:

♦ Chilled Coupe Glass

METHOD:

1. Fill a mixing glass with ice.

2. Add the bourbon, vermouth, bitters and syrup and stir for 30 seconds.

3. Strain into the chilled coupe.

4. Garnish with cherry and serve.

HINTS AND TIPS:

Use flavoured bitters instead of orange syrup for depth of flavour.

SAZERAC

The Sazerac is said to be the oldest whisky-based cocktail. The story goes that the Sazerac was invented by an apothecary called Antoine Peychaud in 1838. The recipe has changed over time and there are many variables in the different recipes you will find in cocktail mixing books. We have selected a recipe that is a historical journey, using most of the ingredients that have been altered or discarded over time.

INGREDIENTS:

♦ Absinthe to rinse (10 ml // 1/3 oz)

♦ Chilled Water (60 ml // 2 oz)

♦ Bourbon Whisky (20 ml // 2/3 oz)

♦ Rye Whisky (20 ml // 2/3 oz)

♦ Cognac (15 ml // ½ oz)

♦ Sugar Syrup (10ml // 1/3 oz)

♦ Standard Bitters, 4 dashes

♦ 1 Sugar Cube

♦ Water, tablespoon

GARNISH:

♦ Lemon Twirl

GLASS AND ICE:

♦ Rocks Glass, chilled

METHOD:

1. Rinse a chilled rocks glass with absinthe and set aside.

2. Add the water, sugar cube and bitters to a mixing glass and muddle.

3. Fill the mixing glass with ice.

4. Add both the bourbon and rye whisky and stir until chilled, about 20 seconds.

5. Strain over the absinthe rinsed glass.

6. Add the lemon twirl garnish and serve.

HINTS AND TIPS:

If you don't want to spend the money on absinthe, you can rinse the glass with a less expensive herb-based liquor alternative instead.

MINT JULEP

A Mint Julep was first created for medical use to settle a bad stomach. Spearmint was the traditional mint to be used when it kicked off as a trending cocktail of the American South in the 18th Century.

INGREDIENTS:

- ◆ Bourbon whisky (60 ml // 2 oz)
- ◆ Sugar Cubes, 2
- ◆ Fresh mint leaves, 10

GARNISH:

- ◆ Sprig of mint

GLASS AND ICE:

- ◆ Julep cup or Collins glass
- ◆ Crushed Ice
- ◆ Short Straw

♦ Nb: This drink is traditionally served in an iced silver or pewter cup, but any cold glass will do.

METHOD:

1. Put the mint leaves and sugar into cold cup/glass and muddle well.

2. Add the bourbon.

3. Fill the glass with crushed ice and stir for 20 seconds.

4. Garnish with a sprig of mint and serve with a short straw.

HINTS AND TIPS:

Juleps can be made in a variety of flavours. Mix in a flavoured liquor of your choice and a matching garnish to finish it off. You may also want to add frozen fruit instead of or as well as your crushed ice to create a better effect.

Double the recipe and serve in a long glass with crushed ice to create a summer-time drink for a garden party.

WHISKY MAC

Colonel Hector Mac Donald invented the Whisky Mac. He was nicknamed 'Fighting Mac' and thought of as a hero by Victorian school children. He was serving in occupied India in the time of British rule around 1899. The soldiers around him were drinking ginger wine to ward off cholera, and it is said that he mixed a dram of whisky with his – thus inventing the Whisky Mac.

INGREDIENTS:

- Scotch Whisky (60 ml // 2 oz)

- Ginger Wine (45 ml // 1 ½ oz)

GARNISH:

- None – This drink speaks for itself.

GLASS AND ICE:

- Rocks Glass

- Ice Cubes

METHOD:

1. Pour the whisky and ginger wine directly into the glass.

2. Stir for 10 seconds.

3. Serve.

HINTS AND TIPS:

If you want to spice this up, add more whisky. If you want to sweeten it, add more ginger wine. This is a simple cocktail best served the way Whisky Mac intended!

RUM BASED COCKTAIL RECIPES

Rum based cocktails existed before the term cocktail was even coined. They originated in the Caribbean where rum was made with a high proof. It was then mixed with water, or coconut milk to soften the blow before locals added fresh lime juice to balance the flavours.

Nowadays, rum is a popular drink for cocktails due to its rich flavours, and the fact that you get dark and light rum. In this chapter, we will show you how to prepare delicious rum cocktails designed to bring out the flavours as you drink them.

PINA COLADA

The Pina Colada came from Puerto Rico when a bartender named Ramon Marrero created this fun summer drink in 1954 for excited hotel guests at the Caribe Hilton hotel.

INGREDIENTS:

- White Rum (60 ml // 2 oz)
- Cream of Coconut (100 ml // 3 ½ oz)
- Pineapple Juice (100 ml // 3 ½ oz)
- Fresh Lime Juice (15 ml // ½ oz)

GARNISH:

- Pineapple Wedge
- Coconut Wedge

GLASS AND ICE:

- Poco Grande or High Ball Glass
- Pebble or crushed ice

METHOD:

1. Fill shaker with ice.

2. Add rum, coconut cream and pineapple juice with fresh lime juice and shake for 20 seconds.

3. Strain over glass filled with pebble or crushed ice.

4. Garnish with pineapple or coconut wedge on the side of the glass.

5. Serve.

HINTS AND TIPS:

A pina colada is supposed to be a fun drink. Why not add a small cocktail umbrella or other fun frippery for added joy?

You can also add frozen pineapple chunks or cherries to give it that extra something special.

MOJITO

The birth of the Mojito could have been as early as the 1500s, when Sir Francis Drake turned to the locals in Havana to help treat his crew that had dysentery. They came aboard his ship with a cure of mint leaves, the juice from sugar cane and lime juice. After this a drink called 'El Draque', which was very similar to the modern Mojito, was very popular in the area. Another story of the Mojito's origins is a bar in Havana called La Bodeguita Del Medio. A popular theory is that the African people who were enslaved to work in Cuban sugar fields invented this drink.

INGREDIENTS:

- ◆ White Rum (60 ml // 2 oz)

- ◆ Fresh Lime Juice (10 ml // 1/3 oz)

- ◆ Simple Syrup (15 ml // 1/2 oz)

- ◆ Fresh mint leaves, 10

- ◆ Club Soda

GARNISH:

- ◆ Lime twist or wedge

- ◆ Sprig of Mint

GLASS AND ICE:

- ♦ Collins/Highball Glass
- ♦ Ice Cubes

METHOD:

1. Add the mint and simple syrup to a shaker and muddle.

2. Add the rum, lime and fill the shaker with ice.

3. Shake for 10 seconds.

4. Strain into glass and add fresh ice cubes.

5. Pour club soda to top.

6. Garnish with mint sprig and lime twist/wedge, depending on your preference.

HINTS AND TIPS:

The Mojito is traditionally made in a tall glass. Many bartenders have been making it in rocks glasses and serving over crushed ice with a straw. It makes for a refreshing summer cocktail and means that this recipe will stretch to at least two servings.

Mojitos come in many flavours. They are a bartender's favourite to mix up and change for complete customer satisfaction. Why not try adding salt or some bitter flavours to the drink and see how you like it?

DAIQUIRI

The Daiquiri's invention is evidenced by a cocktail recipe card that is signed by the inventor himself in 1896. Jennings Cox was holding a cocktail party in Cuba. It is said that upon running out of gin he used rum instead and thus, the beloved Daiquiri was born. This cocktail was likely drunk in Cuba before he wrote it down – due to the mass availability of the ingredients. However, it is a great story!

INGREDIENTS:

♦ White Rum (60 ml // 2 oz)

♦ Fresh lime juice (30 ml // 1 oz)

♦ Two Brown Sugar Cubes

GARNISH:

♦ Lime twist

GLASS AND ICE:

♦ Chilled coupe glass

METHOD:

1. Add the rum and fresh lime juice to an iced cocktail shaker and shake for 30 seconds.

2. Strain into your chilled coupe glass.

3. Stir in your sugar cubes.

4. Add lime twist garnish.

5. Serve immediately.

HINTS AND TIPS:

You can use mascarpone sugar syrup for a greater depth of flavour, or sugar syrup.

STRAWBERRY DAIQUIRI

Daiquiris are one of the most popular cocktails in the world. They are well known for coming in all kinds of flavours with added fruits and syrups. There seems to be no end to the possibilities with these drinks. Making a frozen cocktail is simple and very fast to achieve with a blender. Follow this recipe for a delicious treat on a hot summer's afternoon.

INGREDIENTS:

- White rum (90 ml // 3 oz)
- Frozen strawberries (100 g // ½ cup)
- Fresh strawberries (100 g // ½ cup)
- Fresh lime juice (30 ml // 1 oz)
- Simple syrup (45 ml // 1 ½ oz)

GARNISH:

- Small whole strawberry

GLASS AND ICE:

- Chilled double bowl glass

METHOD:

1. Blend the strawberries taking care to select one of the fresh ones for your garnish.

2. Strain through a sieve to remove some of the seeds.

3. Add the blended strawberries, rum, lime juice and simple syrup to the blender and pulse a few times.

4. Pour into a chilled Margarita glass

5. Cut a slit in your strawberry and place on the side of your glass as a garnish.

6. Serve immediately.

HINTS AND TIPS:

Now you know how to make a great frozen daiquiri, why not try it with some more outrageous flavours? Mango Daiquiris are delicious or even a grape-based Daiquiri but remember to take the skins off the grapes before blending.

RUM AND GINGERS

This no-nonsense cocktail originated after the first world war.

INGREDIENTS:

♦ Dark Rum (60 ml // 2 oz)

♦ Ginger Beer to top

♦ Fresh Lime Juice (30 ml // 1 oz)

GARNISH:

♦ Lime Wedge

♦ Sugared Ginger

GLASS AND ICE:

♦ Traditional Chilled copper mug or a Collins Glass

♦ Ice Cubes / Crushed Ice

METHOD:

1. Add ice cubes to Collins glass.

2. Add the lime juice and rum and stir with a stirring spoon.

3. Fill to top with ginger beer.

4. Add a lime wedge and sugared ginger and serve.

HINTS AND TIPS:

The type of ginger beer that you use in this drink makes all the difference. Find one that is well carbonated with a deep flavour. Alcoholic ginger beer makes this cocktail far more potent, while an alcohol-free alternative leads to a more refreshing experience. Make sure the ginger beer does not contain too much sugar or sweetener. If you find the cocktail too sweet, add a little more lime juice.

VODKA BASED COCKTAIL RECIPES

Vodka is most often made from potatoes. It can also come from grains, molasses or other products that can be distilled to create alcohol. The first evidence of the existence of vodka was in the early 1400s when it appeared in a manuscript from Poland. There are arguments as to exactly where it originated but it is definitely Eastern Europe. Perhaps Poland, Finland or Russia. Russia was first used as a medicine, it was said that it warded off the cold. It was not until the ascension of Catharine the Great in 1762 that it became a popular, high-class distilled alcohol. The Russian Nobel men found a way to purify the drink through charcoal. After the Russian Revolution, many citizens left Russia and brought their knowledge of vodka with them, and this was the start of its huge popularity across the western world.

MOSCOW MULE

In 1939 a man named John G. Martin tried to sell vodka to the Americans. They were having none of it, preferring their staples of whisky and rum. He was ready to give up on the venture when he had a chat with his good friend, Wes Price at the Cock and Bull Bar in Los Angeles.

Wes had a big backlog of ginger beer that he couldn't sell either. The pair combined the two and began selling them as Moscow Mules due to their big 'kick'. Shortly after they had started selling them, a young Russian woman, Sophie Berezinski, came to the bar with a deal to sell them copper mugs. The copper kept the drink colder for longer and became a great selling point.

Martin travelled America with a polaroid camera taking photos of bartenders making Moscow Mules in copper mugs. At each new bar he would take two photos, one for the bartender to put on the wall and one for himself to add to his sales collection.

INGREDIENTS:

- ◆ Vodka (60 ml // 2 oz)

- ◆ Fresh lime juice (15 ml // ½ oz)

- ◆ Ginger beer to top

GARNISH:

♦ Wedge of lime

GLASS AND ICE:

♦ Collins glass

♦ Ice Cubes

METHOD:

| 1. | Fill Collins glass with ice. |

| 2. | Add all the ingredients and stir well. |

HINTS AND TIPS:

Add 1 oz of ginger wine to increase the potency of the Moscow Mule.

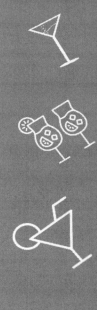

BLOODY MARY

The Bloody Mary is an all-time classic cocktail. It is a personal, customisable drink that each person, like a fingerprint, prefers in a slightly different way. There are many recipes for complex Bloody Marys. We will start simple and classic so that you can build on it how you wish as you become an experienced home-mixologist. Ferdinand Petiot claimed the invention of the Bloody Mary in a hotel bar in Paris in 1934. He added the idea of spice to a drink that already existed by a man named George Jessel.

INGREDIENTS:

- Vodka (60 ml // 2 oz)
- Fresh tomato juice (180 ml // 6 oz)
- Black pepper
- Chili sauce

GARNISH:

- A stick of celery
- Two olives

GLASS AND ICE:

- ◆ Highball glass
- ◆ Ice Cubes

METHOD:

1. Add ice to a mixing glass.

2. Add the ingredients to the mixing glass, including vodka, fresh tomato juice, chili sauce and black pepper.

3. Stir well, for about 30 seconds.

4. Strain into a Collins glass with ice cubes.

5. Impale the olives on a cocktail stick and place over the glass, add the celery stick garnish.

6. When serving, invite guests to ask for more hot sauce or black pepper to taste.

HINTS AND TIPS:

You can get creative with a Bloody Mary. From branded sauces to herbs, there are many flavours that you can add to create a deep and delicious tomato-based drink. Horseradish and garlic can be excellent additions. Make sure you always have enough chili sauce if you are serving them for a party.

A Bloody Mary is one of the few cocktails when more is more when it comes to a garnish. Add a sprig of mint, lime wedge and celery leaves to your olive and celery stick garnish. Whatever you think will boost the pleasure of the person drinking it. Serve with chili sauce and black pepper on the table so people can choose the potency of their drink.

WHEN TO SERVE:

Bloody Marys are often drunk to cure a hangover or as a 'hair of the dog' drink at a Sunday brunch. A great serving idea for these is to have a Bloody Mary Tapas Party on a Sunday. Lay the table with an assortment of ingredients that you might add to a Bloody Mary, or as a garnish. Lay out some oily hors d'oeuvres to help soak up the alcohol and have guests enjoy a few hours of making their own Bloody Marys. The perfect, indulgent Sunday afternoon activity.

TEQUILA BASED COCKTAIL RECIPES

Tequila is made from the Agave tequilina plant, a succulent native to Mexico. The bulb of the plant is first baked and then the juices are released. This juice is then fermented to make tequila. It is a common misconception that worms are added to tequila bottles simply for the way it looks. This is actually a nod to the fermentation process of history when worms would live in the bulb and get mixed up into the process and end up in the drink. Tequila.

MARGARITA

The origin of the Margarita is uncertain. Like with many other cocktails, there are a lot of folktales and false stories surrounding it. One is that it was invented in 1938 by a bar owner for his girlfriend named Margarita who was allergic to all alcohol except tequila and loved to put salt in her drinks. A year earlier in a cocktail recipe book, there is a recipe for a margarita under the title of a Picador. Some mixologist historians believe that the margarita could have been from far earlier around the time of prohibition.

INGREDIENTS:

- Tequila (60 ml // 2 oz)
- Orange Liqueur (45 ml // 1 ½ oz) ✓ (to make)
- Fresh Lime Juice (30 ml // 1 oz) + LIMES
- Simple Syrup (15 ml // ½ oz)

GARNISH:

- Lime Ring
- Coarse salt

74

GLASS AND ICE:

- ◆ Double-bowl glass
- ◆ Crushed ice

METHOD:

1. Prepare your double bowl glass by running the lime around the rim. Place your salt in a shallow bowl or on a plate and gently dip the glass into it so that the rim is lightly covered in salt.

2. Add some crushed ice to the glass and place to one side.

3. Half fill a cocktail shaker with ice and add the tequila, orange liqueur, fresh lime juice and simple syrup.

4. Shake for 20 seconds.

5. Strain over the serving glass taking care not to wet the rim.

6. Garnish with lime ring and serve immediately.

HINTS AND TIPS:

You may also wish to garnish the rim of your coupe glass with sugar. Gently dip your glass in water, you can use lime and run it around the rim instead, but it depends on how you want it to taste. Then lightly into a flat base of sugar, it should coat the rim of the glass in an even layer of sugar. Give it 30 seconds to set before adding the cocktail mix.

PALOMA

The origins of the Paloma are unknown. Its first mention was in a popular cocktail-making book in 1953. However, this was found to be the work of tricksters who altered some cocktail recipes on Wikipedia back in 2009. The name 'Paloma' means dove in Spanish. The original recipe calls for grapefruit soda, but we think it tastes much better with some fresh grapefruit juice and soda water

INGREDIENTS:

- Tequila (60 ml // 2 oz)

- Fresh lime juice (15 ml // ½ oz)

- Grapefruit juice (15 ml // ½ oz)

- Soda water to top

GARNISH:

- Lime wedge

- Salt

GLASS AND ICE:

- ◆ Highball glass
- ◆ Crushed ice

METHOD:

1. Salt the rim of the glass (see Margarita recipe for instructions).

2. Set glass aside.

3. Add tequila, fresh lime juice and grapefruit juice to a mixing glass and stir for 20 seconds.

4. Strain over glass.

5. Add lime wedge and pour over soda water to top.

6. Serve.

HINTS AND TIPS:

The Paloma is all about citrus flavours. You can substitute lemon for the lime or blood oranges for the grapefruit.

CHAMPAGNE BASED COCKTAIL RECIPES

Champagne is a base for a cocktail that most people can get on board with. It is as versatile as soda water when it comes to creating marvellous mixes. Of course, you don't need to use champagne. Pick the bubbles of your choice and start creating masterpieces in your home bar.

MIMOSA

This simple cocktail is perfect for breakfast time or brunch. Some say it was invented by Sir Alfred Hitchcock in the 1940s. This is unlikely but did help the Mimosa to gain fame and glory across America. It is likely that it is an adaptation of the popular Bucks Fizz cocktail invented in 1921 at the Buck's Club in London. It was said that the drink gave men an excuse to start drinking before lunch when they visited gentlemen's clubs. Now it gives everyone an excuse to start drinking before lunch in the comfort of their own homes.

INGREDIENTS:

◆ Champagne (90 ml // 3 oz)

◆ Freshly squeezed orange Juice (60 ml // 2 oz)

GARNISH:

◆ Orange wheel

GLASS AND ICE:

◆ Highball Ice

◆ Crushed Ice

METHOD:

1. Add the fresh orange juice straight to your highball glass.

2. Pour over champagne.

3. Add garnish.

4. Serve.

HINTS AND TIPS:

Alter the ratio of champagne to orange juice to suit your taste. This can be a great low alcohol cocktail. If you want to give it a kick add ½ oz of flavoured liqueur of your choice before you add the champagne and give it a slight stir before adding your bubbles to keep them as carbonated as possible.

CHAMPAGNE COCKTAIL

The Champagne Cocktail is a delight to receive at a party. The sugar in it makes the bubbles fizz long after you serve it. A great way to get a cocktail party started or to toast a celebration. The Champagne Cocktail first started in the 1800s though it was served in a very different way to today in a rocks glass over ice. Charles Dickens invented a cocktail which he called 'Tom Gin and Champagne Cups' in which he mixed gin, champagne and lemon. Whoever invented the Champagne Cocktail - it is surely one to take note of for its pure simplistic decadence.

INGREDIENTS:

- ◆ Champagne (150 ml // 5 oz)

- ◆ Bitters, 5 dashes

- ◆ Lemon Skin

GARNISH:

- ◆ Maraschino cherry

GLASS AND ICE:

- ◆ Champagne Flute, chilled

METHOD:

1. Pop a sugar cube in the bottom of the glass.

2. Add five dashes of bitters to the cube of sugar.

3. Squeeze the lemon skin into the glass and rub it around the rim.

4. Pour over the champagne, add the cherry and serve.

HINTS AND TIPS:

This is a fast serve cocktail so always ensure you have any garnish prepared in advance especially if you are using a citrus fruit twist.

FUN COCKTAILS

Cocktails aren't meant to be serious. As a home mixologist, you can create all sorts of wild and wonderful works of art as you grow in your understanding of style and flavour. Matching flavours can lead to some truly astonishing creations. Add fripperies to your cocktails to create sparkling, colourful masterpieces. In this next section, we will show you some traditionally fun cocktails for you to try at home which should give you the inspiration to try some more of your own.

When it comes to fun cocktails ensure that you give the shaker an extra wild shake and be attentive to your guests. Getting a big, exciting cocktail is a real treat and if you do it right you will have some very satisfied friends at your party!

Indulge in the whimsy!

LONG ISLAND ICED-TEA

Named after its colour rather than its flavour the Long Island Iced tea is a potent drink and one that bartenders dislike making during busy periods for the amount of pouring that goes into it. It was popularised in the 1970s but little is known about its origin. It could have been at a cocktail-making competition or tentative prohibition drinkers wanting to disguise their alcohol.

INGREDIENTS:

- Tequila (20 ml // 2/3 oz)

- Gin (20 ml // 2/3 oz)

- Vodka (20 ml // 2/3 oz)

- Rum (20 ml // 2/3 oz)

- Triple Sec (20 ml // 2/3 oz)

- Simple Syrup (20 ml // 2/3 oz)

- Fresh Lemon Juice (20 ml // 2/3 oz)

- Cola to top

GARNISH:

- Lemon wedge

GLASS AND ICE:

- ◆ Collins Glass
- ◆ Ice Cubes

METHOD:

| 1. | Add all alcoholic ingredients, the simple syrup and the lemon juice to a cocktail shaker with ice. |

| 2. | Shake well for 20 seconds. |

| 3. | Strain over the Collins glass. |

| 4. | Add coke to top. |

| 5. | Garnish with lemon wedge and serve. |

HINTS AND TIPS:

There are many variations to the Long Island. However, it should always contain no fewer than five spirits.

SEX ON THE BEACH

Sex on the Beach was said to be invented by a man named Ted Pizio trying to sell peach schnapps to those on spring break in Florida. However, there were mentions of a drink very similar to the cocktail in cocktail books in 1982.

INGREDIENTS:

- Vodka (30 ml // 1 oz)
- Peach schnapps (30 ml // 1 oz)
- Cranberry juice (60 ml // 2 oz)
- Fresh orange juice (60 ml // 2 oz)

GARNISH:

- Frozen cranberries

GLASS AND ICE:

- Highball glass
- Ice Cubes

METHOD:

1. Add the vodka, schnapps and cranberry juice to a cocktail shaker and shake for 20 seconds.

2. Strain over the highball glass.

3. Gently pour in the orange juice over the top.

4. Add garnish and serve.

HINTS AND TIPS:

Add blackcurrant schnapps for a deeper flavour. If you want a more traditional cocktail, sub the cranberry juice for grenadine and pour it in before you pour over the mix.

COSMOPOLITAN

Neal Murrey a bartender at a steak house in New York lays claim to the cosmopolitan. He says that he invented it, and handed it to a customer who exclaimed 'how cosmopolitan' and hence that is how the drink got its name.

INGREDIENTS:

- ◆ Vodka (60 ml // 2 oz)
- ◆ Cranberry juice to top
- ◆ Fresh lime juice (30 ml // 1 oz)

GARNISH:

- ◆ Maraschino cherry

GLASS AND ICE:

- ◆ Cocktail glass

METHOD:

1. Add the vodka, cranberry and lime juice to your shaker and shake for 30 seconds.

2. Strain over the cocktail glass.

3. Add maraschino cherry on a cocktail stick.

4. Serve.

HINTS AND TIPS:

To give this recipe an extra kick you can add orange liqueur. Double up the recipe and add to a highball glass with crushed ice for a fantastic summer cocktail. Cosmos are also great served in jugs at a springtime party to share with a big group. When serving in a jug add plenty of ice cubes to keep the drink cool before it is served.

BIKE AND SIDECAR

This is a Sidecar cocktail with a tequila twist. Adapted from the original, this is a long drink to be served at garden festivities and for the adventurous person at the party.

INGREDIENTS:

- Cognac (60 ml // 2 oz)
- Tequila (45 ml // 1 ½ oz)
- Orange liqueur (30 ml // 1 oz)
- Fresh lemon juice (20 ml // 2/3 oz)
- Simple syrup (15 ml // ½ oz)
- Soda to top

GARNISH:

- Orange Wheel

GLASS AND ICE:

- Highball glass

♦ Crushed ice

METHOD:

1. Add the alcohol, lemon juice and simple syrup to a cocktail shaker and shake for 20 seconds.

2. Strain over the Highball glass.

3. Pour soda water to top.

4. Garnish with orange wheel.

5. Serve

HINTS AND TIPS:

To make an original sidecar remove the tequila, simple syrup and soda water and serve in a coupe glass with a sugared rim and a maraschino cherry garnish.

NON-ALCOHOLIC COCKTAIL RECIPES

A non-alcoholic cocktail should be made with the same, if not more, flourish than the alcoholic. Know your audience. If it is a pregnant woman who is itching for a drink but can't have one, give her as many garnishes as possible and make it look like the most special cocktail in the world. If it is someone who simply does not drink, they might prefer a discretely non-alcoholic drink.

The great thing about being a home mixologist is that you already know the people coming to your house and can be prepared. If there are children coming, always have cocktail umbrellas at the ready. When making an alcohol-free cocktail it can be a good idea to ask your friend whether they want it to taste like alcohol or more of a fruity drink.

If your guests are ordering a non-alcoholic version of the same drink that others are drinking, have a distinguishable garnish that you only use for non-alcoholic drinks. This will ensure that the person you're serving doesn't get a nasty surprise.

If you want to make a cocktail taste alcoholic without too much alcohol, you can always use a couple of drops of bitters in your mocktail. Always check that the person you are making it for is ok with this as it does contain alcohol even if it is only a small amount. You can also add lime and tonic water to get a similar effect without the alcohol.

VIRGIN PINA COLADA

INGREDIENTS:

- Coconut milk (90 ml // 3 oz)

- Pineapple Juice to top

- Ice Cream (2 scoops)

- Fresh Lime Juice (15 ml // ½ oz)

- Rum flavouring (2 drops)

GARNISH:

- Pineapple wedge

- Cocktail umbrella

- Maraschino cherry

GLASS AND ICE:

- Poco Grande

METHOD:

1. Add coconut milk, pineapple juice, lime juice and rum flavouring to an iced cocktail shaker and shake for 20 seconds.

2. Scoop ice cream into Poco Grande glass.

3. Strain mix from cocktail shaker into the glass.

4. Garnish with a flourish and serve.

HINTS AND TIPS:

You can leave out the lime and the rum flavouring if you want the drink to taste sweeter. Add sugar syrup to take the sugar buzz up a notch.

FAIRY-TALE BLUSH

An invention that gets its name from every princess that has ever been kissed. Invented in 2021 by a discerning barmaid, this drink is sure to be a big hit with the alcohol-free crowd.

INGREDIENTS:

♦ Cranberry juice (120 ml // 4 oz)

♦ Freshly squeezed lime juice (15 ml // ½ oz)

♦ Freshly squeezed lemon juice (15 ml // ½ oz)

♦ Ginger syrup (15 ml // ½ oz)

♦ Soda water to top

GARNISH:

♦ Mint leaves

♦ Frozen cranberries

♦ Lime wedge

GLASS AND ICE:

- ♦ Collins glass
- ♦ Crushed ice

METHOD:

1. Add the cranberry, lime and lemon juice and the ginger syrup to an iced cocktail shaker and shake for 20 seconds.

2. Add the frozen cranberries, mint leaves and crushed ice to the Collins glass.

3. Strain the mix into the Collins glass and muddle for 10 seconds.

4. Pour over the soda water to top.

5. Garnish with a lime wedge and serve.

HINTS AND TIPS:

You can make a blended, sweeter version of this by blending frozen strawberries and adding them to the drink.

THE SPA

The Spa is a refreshing mocktail. Relax and enjoy as it washes over your body like an ocean over a desert's sands. Designed to cool, awaken and freshen up the discerning drinker.

INGREDIENTS:

- Fresh lime juice (90 ml // 3 oz)

- Simple syrup (15 ml // ½ oz)

- Cucumber, peeled and sliced

- Fresh mint

- Fresh peppermint

- Soda water to top

GARNISH:

- Cucumber wheel

- Sprig of peppermint

- Celery stick

GLASS AND ICE:

- Collins glass, chilled

- Ice Cubes

- Spoon

METHOD:

1. Add the lime juice, simple syrup, cucumber, mint and peppermint to a mixing glass and muddle well to release the flavours.

2. Transfer into a cocktail shaker with ice and shake for 20 seconds.

3. Strain over Collins glass and add the cucumber, peppermint and celery garnish.

4. Serve with a mixing spoon.

HINTS AND TIPS:

You can leave out the simple syrup if you want a tarter cocktail. If you want a spicy kick, add a few drops of chili sauce when you serve.

CONCLUSION

You have reached the end of The Original Cocktail Book! By now, you should feel like a professional home mixologist. Consider what you have learned on this journey. Do you look at flavour differently? Are you cocktail obsessed? Maybe your parties are now the talk of all of your friends. Or perhaps you have had many a perfect date night with that special someone over a Tom Collins. Whatever you have used your new mixology superpowers for, I hope that you have enjoyed reading this compilation of recipes and learning more about how to mix a delicious cocktail at home. There are several pages in the back of this book for you to add your own recipes. Why not take your favourite spirit and try and make a delicious cocktail out of it. Or if you prefer, give a mocktail a go and see what you can do to make the flavours bounce out of the glass and into your mouth. You are now ready to take this next step in your journey towards being a home bartender. Remember to always taste what you make to ensure quality and always make your cocktails with finesse and love to get the best results!

WRITE YOUR OWN RECIPES

RECIPE:

RECIPE:

....

....

....

....

....

....

....

....

....

....

....

....

....

....

RECIPE:

....

....

....

....

....

....

....

....

....

....

....

....

....

....

....

RECIPE:

....
....
....
....
....
....
....
....
....
....
....
....
....
....
....
....
....
....
....
....

RECIPE:

....

....

....

....

....

....

....

....

....

....

....

....

....

....

....

DISCLAIMER

This book contains opinions and ideas of the author and is meant to teach the reader informative and helpful knowledge while due care should be taken by the user in the application of the information provided. The instructions and strategies are possibly not right for every reader and there is no guarantee that they work for everyone. Using this book and implementing the information/recipes therein contained is explicitly your own responsibility and risk. This work with all its contents, does not guarantee correctness, completion, quality or correctness of the provided information. Misinformation or misprints cannot be completely eliminated.

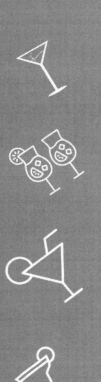

Printed in Great Britain
by Amazon